Touchwood

Poetry by Dick Davis

In the Distance

Seeing the World

The Covenant

Devices and Desires
NEW AND SELECTED POEMS 1967–1987

In Translation

Attar: The Conference of the Birds
with Afkham Darbandi

Ferdowsi: The Legend of Seyavash

Borrowed Ware
MEDIEVAL PERSIAN EPIGRAMS

Anvil Press **Review Slip**

The publishers have pleasure in sending for review a copy of

DICK DAVIS

Touchwood

ISBN 0 85646 269 1
£7.95 80pp
7 November 1996

and would appreciate a copy of any notice that appears.

For further information please contact

ANVIL PRESS POETRY LTD
Neptune House 70 Royal Hill London SE10 8RT
TEL. 0181 469 3033 FAX. 0181 469 3363
E-MAIL anvil@cix.compulink.co.uk

DICK DAVIS

Touchwood

ANVIL PRESS POETRY

Published in 1996
by Anvil Press Poetry Ltd
69 King George Street London SE10 8PX

This book is published
with financial assistance from
The Arts Council of England

Designed and composed by Anvil
Photoset in Plantin by Typestream
Printed and bound in England
by The Arc & Throstle Press, Todmorden, Lancs
Distributed by Password, Manchester

ISBN 0 85646 269 1

A catalogue record for this book
is available from the British Library

ACKNOWLEDGEMENTS

Some of these poems have appeared in *Cambridge Review*, *Epigrammatist*, *la fontana*, *PN Review*, *Threepenny Review*, *Sewanee Review* and *Yale Review*. 'A Sasanian Palace' appeared as a broadsheet published by Bernard Stone and Raymond Danowski, The Turret Bookshop, London.

To John Gibson

TEACHER AND FRIEND

'TOUCHWOOD: *decayed wood . . .*
used as tinder.'

Contents

1

To 'Eshqi

1893–1924, Iranian poet, murdered by his country's secret police

I'm someone who you wouldn't want to know.
If I had met you eighty years ago
Before my birth, your death, I hardly think
That we'd have trusted, even sensed, the link
That I sense now, in reading you, between
Your youth and mine – too much would intervene.
My accent would be just a goad to you
To spit, or run, or tell me all you knew
Of England's avarice and treachery.
I've heard that mix of fact and fantasy
And met your avatars so many times,
Sat listening to the litany of crimes –
Been patient, lost my temper, smiled, agreed,
And always recognized that clawing need
To spell the rape out once again, to say
'We were your helpless and dismembered prey.'
I'm used by now to acting out the son
The fathers' sins are visited upon –
Imputed sins or true, it's all the same:
The ache is real enough, and so's the blame.

What could unite us then? What quirk could span
The chasm cast between an Englishman,
A wandering subject of that nation state
Your patriotic confrères love to hate,
And you whose life was given to the fight
To free all Asia from imperial might?

First there's the wandering – like me you spent
Long years in self-elected banishment,
In cities where your language was a way
To discount everything you had to say,
To mark you as a parasite or worse –

Was this the prod that pushed you into verse?
The sudden sense that language is a maze,
That meaning mystifies, that sound betrays?
And then the sense that if this sense were true
You might as well exploit what threatened you?
Above all, words themselves, and poetry –
I see in you what I once felt in me,
A kind of drunkenness for what the past
And language lend us, and which will not last,
A pointless love for sound and sense allied,
Bequeathed by all the poets who have died.
And there's the feeling too your young verse gives
Of one who's fearful of the way he lives,
Who's hounded by the thought of death, whose need
For it is like a harsh erotic greed –
Till revelling in your grief you prophesied
That soon enough you would embrace the bride:
A murderer's bullet made your rhetoric
Appear as sober as arithmetic.

By contrast my more circumspect flirtation
With Thanatos avoided consummation:
But still your verse revives for me that sense
Of self-inflicted psychic violence,
A mayhem of the spirit that destroyed
My youth and left a suicidal void . . .
Enough of that; that I survived is due
To someone like and wholly unlike you.

Are these enough then? Verse and exile, death,
Common humanity; shared, human breath?
Why should I look for a response from you?
Why should I care? No words can now undo
The violence of your life and of its end,
And what can reach you from a would-be friend?
Not language, not these verses that I make
In spite of silence for your verses' sake:

Dear poet, here, too late, is sympathy,
Late friendship from a helpless enemy –
An unavailing monologue, but made
In homage to your absent, angry shade.

A Monorhyme for Miscegenation

for Yass Amir-Ebrahimi and Stuart Benis

We all know what our elders warned
In their admonitory drone,

'Water and oil won't mix, my child –
Play safe, stick staunchly to your own.'

And I concede they're half right when
I think of all the pairs I've known

(Black / White, Jew / Gentile, Moslem / Me –
The home-raised with the foreign-grown):

Mixed marriages, it's true, can make
Two lives a dire disaster zone.

But only half: since when they work
(As my luck, and my friends', has shown)

Their intricate accommodations
Make them impossible to clone:

For gross, *gemütlich* kindness, for
Love's larky, lively undertone,

For all desired and decent virtues,
They stand astonished and alone.

Given Back, After Illness

Again after absence
You are home, but weak, chastened,
Come now to be cherished
Among flowers and our children,
As loved and as longed for
As they were new born.

Again after absence
You're beguiled by such beauty,
But worn now and wasted
In a world too unwieldy,
Wanting sleep and long silence
For hour after hour.

Again after absence
Your head presses our pillows
And I wake by your profile
Cut clean as a coin's face,
There to breathe in the breath
You frailly exhale.

After the Angels

Once the angels had dispersed
Diaphanous into
The starry nebulae,
Men asked the animals
For versions of themselves.

So many choices waited:
Loners and lethal packs,
Slow vultures, sly hyenas
That scavenge other lives,
Grand solitaries like
The bear that never seeks
Its kind except to mate,
The spider spinning death
For all unwary insects,
Cold-water fish that dive
Into the darker depths
Loving the icy reaches,
If we can call that chill
Beyond all passion love.

And there were those like us
Who scavenged too, for comfort –
Anthropomorphic, schmaltzy,
Happy to see the monkeys
Defleaing one another,
Cuffing, hugging, their babies.

Happy to see two ducks
Bobbing downstream from us
Alert for scraps we throw them,
Their movements weirdly twinned
Together and together,

Solicitous and greedy,
Snapping up what's offered –
The pretty mandarin ducks
That pair off once, for life.

Still

Still after twenty years I keep
    Love poems by the bed,
Still when I wake from wandering sleep
    A child's unfinished dread

Empties my body and I turn
    To see your sleeping face –
Wise with a wisdom I can't learn,
    Trusting, giving, in place.

Your Children Growing

You see your own face with another mind
And then your own mind with another face;
You and not you, too raw, then too refined,
A shameful sameness and a stranger's grace.

Comfort

Insomnia: I get up, read, then write,
A bit of consciousness alone at night.
The house is cold; after an hour or two
I stumble back to darkness, warmth and you.
You are asleep but as I gingerly
Edge into bed, you turn to welcome me:
No comfort I have known in any place
Can equal that oblivious embrace.

Into Care

Here is a scene from forty years ago:
A skinny, snivelling child of three or so

Sits on a table, naked and shamefaced.
A woman dabs his body to the waist

With yellow pungent ointment and he feels
Her shock as she remarks, 'Look at the weals

On this boy's back.' Her colleague steps across:
Gently she touches him. He's at a loss

To think what kind of 'wheels' she sees, but knows
That here at least there will be no more blows.

Pragmatic Therapy

Old childhood traumas must come out they say –
Dig down, prise loose, let in the light of day.

You found a rusted nail stuck in a door,
Tugged, wrestled with the pliers, fumed and swore

Until it snapped – and left a jagged pin
Lying in wait to snag unwary skin.

What could you do but bang it home? You hit
The thing with all your strength and buried it.

Touchwood

Quirks of lost childhood give
The fears by which we live,
And look – identity
Is like this twisted tree
The lightning struck at there,
Till for a dry, warm lair
The woodlice entered it:
In secret, bit by bit,
They make a mealy bin
Of touchwood sealed within.

Anthony 1946–1966

Brother, now that you are dead
And live only in my head
Where your life is as the sound
Of deep water underground
Moving with its steady roar
Like the silence we ignore
As the given of our being,
As the daylight to our seeing;
Brother, though there is no way
You can hear the words I say
Still through more than twenty years
I ask pardon for your tears –
For the grief that bludgeoned you
And the death it dragged you to,
Knowing, now you cannot live,
You cannot forget, forgive,
Knowing unforgiven I
Must live on and fear to die.

A Photograph of Two Brothers

How old were we? Eight, ten or so?
I seem the tearful one – you glow,
All bounce and boyish confidence,
Which looking back now makes no sense.
I haven't changed that much – and yes,
I hurt too easily I guess,
Though mostly now the tears I shed
Are proxy tears, for you, long dead.

The Suicide

Here is the punishment, the condign shame,
The frightened child unravelling through the years;
Here is Rejection and the Parlour Game
Whose rules say 'Everything must end in Tears.'

Aftershocks

At nervous intervals
    You feel the pain again,
A jolt of recognition
    Coming God knows when;

And though each time you see
    The tremors have diminished,
You know you'll never say
    'They're over now; it's finished.'

May

Late in the evening light
Grass verge and hedgerow glisten
With one unvarying white;

White cow-parsley below,
Above white hawthorn blossom;
Who in this dusk could know

Where weed to flower gives way,
Or when their ghost releases
The last light of the day?

Going Home

What can be called evasion?
Is it to go away?
Or to ignore the world
And like a limpet stay

Stuck to the self-same rock?
Whichever you decide
– Resistance to the waves,
Surrender to the tide –

What you will not evade
Is doubt accusing you
Of infinite evasion
In all you say and do.

A Sasanian Palace

The great hall at Firuzabad
    Lies open to the weather –
I saw two adolescents there
    Playing chess together.

There was no splendour to distract them;
    Only a cavernous shade
Cast by the drab and crumbling vault
    Where silently they played.

So much of Persian verse laments
    The transience of things
And triteness was mere truth as they
    Pursued each others' kings

Where kings had given orders for
    Armies to march on Rome,
And where I watched their game awhile
    At home, and far from home.

Flight

After the Arab defeat of the Persians in the seventh century AD some aristocrats of the defeated Sasanian dynasty fled to China. Gravestones indicate that they hung on there as a distinct community for at least two centuries.

In time the temporary withdrawal
Became a way of life. How long
Before they could admit there'd be
No going back, before they ceased
To live off rumours of a prince,
A scion of the royal house
In hiding, living hand to mouth,
About to gather troops to hurl
The haughty enemy back from
The gates of Ctesiphon –
                                        which was
A pilfered ruin, a harmless tourists'
Curiosity somewhere beyond
The brave new city of Baghdad?

So they erect the stone inscribed
With words that speak to home though home
Has long since ceased to speak such words,
A witness to a way of life
Corroded by fidelity
That is a kind of willing madness;
A story told and then retold,
Whose referents are all elsewhere,
And now lives only in these minds
That still repeat the litany
Of what was lost, till they too die.

Gold

Its atavistic glitter will not fade
And that's the point: barbaric power and pride
(Piled torques and rhytons gaudy in a grave)
Point to the presence of what lived and died.

Thin gold paint flaking where the panel rots
Beneath a saint's robe and a Duccio sky
Signal not merely bourgeois amour-propre,
But hope that something of us will not die.

Take it as frozen threnody, a sign
Of avid and abashed humility,
Of human failings fined down to the wish
To lodge a fragment in eternity.

Mirak

Mirak, descendant of the Prophet, born
About the middle of the fifteenth century:
An Afghan brought up to the family trade
Of bow-maker, who as an adolescent
Turned to reciting the Qoran, was soon
A praised professional at it, tried his hand
As a calligrapher and thence became
The painter of all painters, the miniaturist
To end them all, the Wonder of the Age,
The unsurpassed whom kings sought out, who sketched
From life – while travelling, while a guest at banquets,
Untroubled whether courtiers crowded him
Or left him to his own absorbed devices;
And to the admiration of his time
Was never seen to use an easel. A man
Whose passion when not painting was for wrestling
(Each day he lifted weights to build his strength)
At which, of course, in due course, he excelled.

A talented young orphan came to him
To be apprenticed as his servant, page,
Paint-mixer, gofer, sweeper-up, a boy
To trace and prick the pounces; now and then
Allowed to colour inexpensive pieces.
This was Behzad, whose teacher Mirak was,
Whose fame eventually eclipsed Mirak's
And whose pure, sumptuous, gentle miniatures,
So bright with passion, whimsy and restraint,
Are now the art's unrivalled masterworks
While not one solitary sheet has been
Attributed with any certainty
To Behzad's quondam teacher – Qoran reciter,
Bow-maker, calligrapher and wrestler,
Mirak, surpassed (perhaps) at last, unheld

By any trade, adept at all he touched,
Patient for mastery but negligent
When once he had the mystery in hand:
Or so we picture him, at this blurred distance.

2

Names

In *Inghilterra* you imagine love
    Voluptuously fair,
A Verdi tenor's voice, the wedding rites
    Of Melos and Despair:

In *Inglistan* exasperated hate,
    A certainty that spies
Corrupt the patient labours of the Just
    With smiles, and gold, and lies:

In *Britain*, as the Mid-West says the word
    (And how much more in *Brit*)
Bemused contempt, respect, a sense that They
    Were, and now We are, It.

And *England*? Childhood's word? Your first flight starts:
    As toy-town falls away
Fear, longing, a voracious hope undo
    Whatever you might say.

We Should Be So Lucky

Here is a shameful, strong
    Nostalgia – to have been
A minor functionary
    At some resplendent scene,

A man trained up in skills
    And complicated rules,
Leaving small room for genius
    And even less for fools,

Someone who knows exactly
    How and what to do,
Who works discreetly, knowing
    Others know this too.

A journeyman musician
    Grimly fuming at
His self-important patrons'
    Catatonic chat;

A portrait painter able –
    Happy – to revoke
Defects of nature with
    A defter, softer stroke;

Or best, court panegyrist,
    Where a perfect rhyme
Might mean a pension paid,
    Perpetually, on time.

Masters

When I was prick-sore young, God knows,
Loose Eros led me by the nose
(Disguised at times as Tenderness
Or worship of pure Comeliness,
But underneath such glozing dress
Lascivious Eros nonetheless).

But now that he's renounced my service
And taught me what polite reserve is,
Am I improved in any way?
– Led by Scholastic Vanity,
Bland, treacherous Timidity:
God give me Eros any day.

Tenured in the Humanities

Now he can live and work among
Those who skim books to write their own,
Who thousand-cut another's tongue
To wag their trophies, clone to clone;

Who when they read are sure that they
Know more than authors what words mean,
Who never opened Rabelais
Though (naturally) they've conned Bakhtin;

Who when they write rewrite their betters
With crowing malice and contempt,
Who mean to trash the mind and letters
(Though they themselves will be exempt) –

A lumpen mob that occupies
The palace and the stable yard,
Whose chief joy is to organize
A long and lucrative *noyade*.

New Reader

He reads, rewriting as he goes – it's just
    A timeless bar-room scene:
'Don't give me that crap,' the bully yells,
    '*I'll* tell you what you mean.'

Art History

Paintings and poems – what survives,
The residue of used-up lives
That want to live a little more.
Their gaze pursues you to the door.

Your life's an orphanage in which
The foundling poor stare at the rich
Who load their arms with children they
Hug briefly – but then walk away.

Epitaph

This erstwhile traveller's
    Become a tourist –
Bring out the fake folk knick-knacks,
    He's no purist.

Serve him his own cuisine
    With an ethnic grin –
Nirvana for him now's
    A Holiday Inn.

Couples

I

Breakfast is brusque and when it's done
Her life without him's rebegun;
She's typing, on the phone, her looks
Say 'I'm preoccupied, these books –
And so much else – need seeing to,
I haven't time to glance at you.'
And all the time what fills his head
Is how she turns to him in bed.

II

Her friends all told her how much he admired her
And naturally she thought that he desired her,
But though he read the books she recommended,
Though her views were the ones that he defended,
Though he accompanied her to exhibitions,
Bought CDs of her favourite musicians,
And proved a prudent person to rely on
For movies, shows, a shoulder there to cry on
(Yes, even that . . .), the move for which she waited
(Expectant, disappointed, then frustrated)
Just never came: and then by God it hit her
(Few truths we have to swallow taste more bitter):
'This bastard who pretends to be so kind
Despises me – he only wants my mind.'

Old Couple

'How much they do,' the neighbours say,
'So kind in any, every way –

So quick to help and never ask
Why they should shoulder one more task.'

Not knowing all they do is for one
Long dead, for whom too little was done.

Middle Age

I

We miss out; we don't mind; we make less fuss.
Living? Our poems can do that for us.

II

Life with no bloom of newness to it;
But, surely now, you always knew it –
That this was how it was to be:
Old friends invited round to tea
At which the rude young are deplored
And no one yawns or says, 'I'm bored.'

Repentance

'I won't do that again,' you say. We'll see.
Tomorrow is another day. Feel free.

Desire

A myth that you believed in once, it's gone
And you can't credit that you've been so stupid:
Damn the whole crew you say, damn Venus, damn
Her sparrows, damn her little bastard Cupid.

A Tease

She'll simper and say, Yes – and go
To meetings hubby never quite suspects,
At which she'll simper and say, No –
Who needs adultery without the sex?

One Kind of Middle-Aged Divorce

They wanted novelty and so split up
Like feral cats in search of feral sex;
Now, trying to climax with a one-night stand,
Each thinks obsessively of his / her ex.

A Qasideh for Edgar Bowers on his Seventieth Birthday

Nasib

X years ago a would-be poet wrote
His mental mentor an egregious note –
Not something of the kind that rock-stars get
(Since he was British and they'd never met)
But still a letter from a serious fan,
Too pushy maybe, glibly partisan
(Of course he sent his own slim volume too
And crossed his fingers, as one never knew . . .):
A cautious note came back – sober, polite,
Gently encouraging the neophyte.

Goriz-gah

I was the jittery, determined fan,
And you the prudent poet; so began
A friendship that has meant as much to me
As any in my nano-Odyssey.

Madh

In Santa Barbara on the well-walked beach,
Talking technique, too moderate to preach
But sure in your perception of the line
Where chaos meets and modifies design;
Or in your room, to me a magic place
Where waves unwove their constant thorough-bass,
A cave of making with an ocean view,
Die Zauberflöte and *The Tempest* too;

Or visiting my family and me
In England where you helped a native see
His homeland with a foreign friendly eye,
Discerning, undeceived, distinctly dry;
Or in Ohio where I write this letter,
Insisting that what's central *can* be better,
In concerts and museums, restaurants, zoos
(These last you seem unable to refuse),
A dear companion with an eye and ear
For all that's complex, marvellous, austere
Or simply filled with an unruly charm –
Whatever will delight and do no harm.
I could not list the things you've taught me here,
The music, paintings, poems, prose – the sheer
Accumulation of delicious stuff
That's in my head because you cared enough
To pass it on – nor could I list the ways
Your casual kindness constantly outweighs
The claims of friendship. Knowing you has been
(And may it be for years yet unforeseen),
To steal a phrase, a liberal education,
A cause for gratitude and celebration.
And if I'd never known you there'd be cause
For more than this inadequate applause
In all you've written – in the poems I
Was all those years ago bowled over by
(My *vade mecum* now and known by heart
They stay my perfect image of the art);
And how much more so in your latest verses
Whose unobtrusive, faultless skill rehearses
Our species' exaltation, need and loss
'Fastened by love upon the human cross'.

Du'a'

I wish you well then, now you've reached the age
It seems appropriate to call you sage –
I doubt sagaciousness will keep you from
The pleasures you pursue with such aplomb,
I hope not anyway. And I trust too
The muse continues to call in on you
And that you'll entertain her and pass on
The gossip that she brings from Helicon.

Qasideh: a praise poem, conventionally in four unequal sections. *Nasib*: introduction. *Goriz-gah*: transition. *Madh*: praise. *Du'a'*: prayer for the object of praise and/or for the writer.

In Praise of Auden

God knows it's possible to fault you
    But of whom worth his salt
And our perusal is this not a given?
    Besides we have to live
Cum grano salis, just as we read you,
    And lives too, like art, can need
Their moments of pure inspired zany.
    For me at least the dull pain
Of our past and present is both conjured
    And distracted by the fun
You so generously heap on our platters,
    A hostess whose old hat
Is outlandish but whose heart beats gracious
    In the spot-on right place.

The cliquey tics that irritated
    Swelled up at a compound rate –
Your campiness and giggly mania
    For the outré and arcane
(I owe *sessile* and *soodling* to your nudges,
    Though a surfeit's like girl-scout fudge
Each meal for a week till one breakfast
    We gasp out, 'Dear hostess, a break!')
Then there's health and religion – two areas
    In which I firmly don't care
To place myself under your tutelage,
    Though glad to be your pupil
In this, if a lollygagging, laggard
    One, now verse is my bag.

How much though you knew, and saw through us . . .
    The schoolmaster's rage to you
Was a small boy's tears, the tyrant's mad gesture
    Nostalgia for the breast

Of mother, O mother, whose Isolde
        You once were to her bold
But decorous Tristan: and how your words waken
        Weeping childhood where we shake
In the grip of the ogres' grand nightmare,
        Bereft of all love and light.
How right too you proved when the doors of Europe
        Slammed to at the word Jew –
Our clerisy's conscience and so branded
        A betrayer of England.

My praise is for decency, craft-lore,
        The twin ways you laughed
Off what wouldn't depart, importunate
        Self-important Fortune,
The hand dealt you by orgulous Duty;
        You could be rude and cute
At the drop of a hat and often
        Were, but the sidelong cough
Of Conscience recalled you always to
        The one life that pays,
As, minding our manners and metres,
        You affirmed the discreet
And distinguished; in cosmic terms a trifle,
        But an unwasted life.

Suzanne Doyle's Poems

The bitter power your poems concentrate
Is like the wines they love to celebrate –
Acrid and sharp, a dark embodiment
Of feral life and earthly sediment,
A tart explosion to the taste and brain
That leaves us reeling and a touch insane,
As if we drank down blood, not something made
By an archaic, honourable trade –
Which is the triumph of the trade, to make
What's tricky and impossible to fake
As wrenching as a hurt child's sudden cry,
As simple as the fact that we will die.

Gossip

imitated from Sa'di, Bustan *Book 7, 3309–3356. Mid 13th century*

Forget the rat-race, hide yourself away
From all the fashion-mongers do and say,
But no one, hermit, hoax or holy Asian,
Can hide from character assassination:
Look, you could be an angel from on high
Cavorting Superman-like in the sky
But still you'd see the slanderers have found
A way to bring you crashing to the ground.
You'll find it easier to keep the menace
Of Adriatic waves away from Venice
Than tie the tattling tongue of someone who
Has homed in on his helpless victim – you!

You choose a life of books and quiet contentment.
Precisely that provokes the brats' resentment,
Whispering in huddles, taking turns to slam you –
Nerd, *Prig*, *Hypocrite*, *Creep* – your virtues damn you.
If someone's shy and finds it hard to be
A social animal perpetually,
They say his strange desire for solitude
Is sanctimonious or downright rude;
If someone likes a laugh and noisy fun
They say he sleeps around with everyone.
If someone's rich they're quick on the attack
Nailing him as an egomaniac,
But if he's poor then he's a sap, a loser,
An irresponsible pan-handling boozer –
On hand to comment on a big-shot's fall
(It shows them there's still justice after all –
'He and his arrogance just had it coming,
So let's see how the bastard likes *real* slumming')
And ready to assault like snarling bitches
Any poor wretch who rises up to riches

('That punks like him succeed is proof that slime
Is all that rises in this rotten time').
If you've a business and it's doing well
Then you're a grasping plutocrat from hell,
But if they see you unemployed they sneer
That cadging meals and money's your 'career'.
You like to talk, you're always on the go,
'Sure, empty vessels make most noise, you know',
The quiet type's 'a frigging bathroom tile,
What's with that condescending silent smile?'
If Turn-the-Other-Cheek's your line they say
'That wimp has got no balls! Him, fight? No way!'
If you're aggressive, though, how they complain –
'I'm out of here, I'm gone, the guy's insane!'
If someone's on a slimmer's scanty diet
The gossips' wagging tongues are never quiet,
But if you like your food, why then of course
You stuff your belly like a hungry horse.
A rich man who lives reasonably they call
A skinflint with no common sense at all,
But if he builds himself a fancy palace
And lives like someone on the set of *Dallas*,
Then he's a tasteless drag-queen or a fool
Who doesn't know that rich kitsch isn't cool.
Someone's a modest stay-at-home, so those
Who change planes oftener than their underclothes
Will say, 'What's he experienced from life,
Tied to the apron of his dumpy wife?'
But if you've seen the world a bit, beware!
A man who's ever travelled anywhere
Is just a drifter who can't settle down,
Meandering pointlessly from town to town.
A bachelor's a loner – when he wakes
At night the lonely bed-frame quakes and shakes,
But married, no one comes to his defence:
His hormones got the better of his sense –
Hot-rodding down the road, he never learned,

And now his Porsche has crashed and overturned.'
An ugly face gets cruelly criticized,
But beauty's just as openly despised
Since envy's first priority's to find
Ways for what's lovely to be undermined.
Once I'd a room-mate who was rather shy,
He seldom smiled or looked you in the eye;
A visitor took me aside and said
'That friend you've got there might as well be dead,
Teach him some manners!' So next day I tried
To put the matter to him as described.
He didn't like it and the argument
Soon threatened to get fairly virulent.
Just then our carping visitor came back;
Immediately he went on the attack
At me! 'Hey, pick on someone your own size,
You've hurt his feelings, now apologize!'
If anger makes you lose your self-possession
You're 'crazy, in the grip of some obsession',
But if you're patient with all comers, then
You're one of those 'soft, wimpy, woos-y' men.
To generous folk they say, 'Hold back, enough,
Tomorrow you'll be begging for the stuff',
To careful spenders though they're sure to say
'What are you saving up for? Judgement Day?'
Enough though, really! Who alive can live
Uncriticized? To be too sensitive
Is self-defeating – as we know, the best
Get even more lambasted than the rest;
The wisest course then's probably to sit
Tight, keep your head down, and put up with it.

A Translator's Nightmare

I think it must have been in Limbo where,
As Dante says, the better poets share
Old friendships, rivalries, once famous fights
And, now they've left it, set the world to rights.
As I was being hustled through in transit
To God knows what damned hole, I thought I'd chance it
And chat to some of the assembled great ones
Who looked as bored as trapped theatre patrons
Who've paid good cash and find they hate the show . . .
I picked on one: 'I rather doubt you know . . .'
He started up and peered at me: 'Know you,
You snivelling fool? Know you? Of course I do!
You ruined my best poem. Look who's here . . .'
He turned to his companions with a sneer,
'Traducer and destroyer of our art,
The biggest stink since Beelzebub's last fart.'
They jostled round, each shouting out his curses,
'You buried me with your insipid verses . . .'
'You left out my best metaphor, you moron . . .'
'You missed my meaning or they set no store on
An accurate rendition where you come from.'
'He comes from where they send the deaf and dumb from,
He got my metre wrong . . .', 'He missed my rhymes',
'He missed puns I don't know how many times,
Then shoved his own in . . .' But I turned and fled,
Afraid that in a moment I'd be dead
A second time, torn limb from spectral limb.

A mist came down and I was lost. A dim
Shape beckoned; thinking it must be my guide,
I ran for reassurance to his side.
But it was someone I'd not seen before,
An old man bent beside the crumbling shore

Of Lethe's stream. He stared a long time, then
'Did you translate?'. I screamed, 'Oh not again!'
But as I backed off one quick claw reached out;
He clutched my coat and with a piercing shout
(He didn't look as though he had it in him)
Cried, 'We've a guest! Who'll be the first to skin him?'
Then added, 'Just my joke now; stay awhile,
The crowd in these parts is quite versatile,
Though we've one thing in common, all of us:
When you were curious, and courteous,
Enough to translate poems from our tongue
All of us gathered here were not among
The chosen ones.' I looked around – a crowd
Now hemmed us in and from it soon a loud
Discordant murmur rose: 'Please, why not mine?'
'You did Z's poems, my stuff's just as fine . . .'
'The greatest critics have admired my verse . . .'
'You worked on crap that's infinitely worse
Than my worst lines.' '*Some* of my stuff's quite good –
You will allow that? – It's not *all* dead wood?
Why then . . . ?' and slowly the reproaches turned
To begging, bragging, angry tears that burned
Their way into my sorry soul.

Once more
I ran and saw my guide, tall on the shore
– The other shore – of Lethe. 'Rescue me!'
I called, 'Get me to where I have to be
For all eternity . . .' He smiled: 'My dear,
You've reached your special hell, it's here. It's here.'

Late

A glass of wine (the third or fourth tonight)
And Hafez read by fire- and candle-light.

Act Two of *Tristan*. As the record plays
German and Persian merge in *Sehnsucht*'s haze.

Now firelight, music, poetry combine
To bless the mind already blurred with wine.

3

Esther

Esther

'Inside the little vaulted room are the two carved wooden coffins, all swathed in damask and brocade. Esther and Mordecai, side by side, and in a little room close by, a beautiful case with the rolls of the Old Testament written on parchment in lovely lettering. And every Friday night the Jews of Hamadan (there are five thousand) gather here, and the book of Esther is read out to them. They seem to be on friendly terms now with the Moslems, but it is only quite recently . . .'

We have: a brave girl and an evil minister
Whose wicked machinations have to fail;
Light triumphs over everything that's sinister –
This story is a cosy fairy-tale.

* * *

We have: a sulky queen who won't play ball,
An underdog who gets his way (of course),
A drunk king with a thousand tarts on call –
This story is a comic tour de force.

* * *

We have: a lunatic of hatred who
Has power to make a people disappear,
Who smiles and stiffens as he murmurs 'Jew' –
This story is the nightmare we most fear.

* * *

Esther and Mordecai, the precious pair
Who worked the system, beat the odds, preserved
A people from the flames the daily news
Now makes us all a party to by proxy

(Mass graves exhumed and anguished recitations
Of Kaddish and Qoran, the Virgin's image
Snug on a rifle-butt – dear talisman
To whisper hatred in a sniper's ear –
The pictures flashed across our greedy media,
Maimed children screaming in a hospital,
A woman's back that pleads for privacy,
Her life eviscerated by her shame;
Bad Faith and Special Pleading, the smug sense that
When our side does it, it's another matter
And doesn't count, I mean they asked for it . . .)

All this, all this long litany of grief
And loathing handed on for generations,
These two averted – who would deny them praise?

* * *

The desert dust and date-palms of Shushan,
Called Shush now, Susa on a Western map:
A hot, sweet, somnolent oasis close
To where a million souls were sundered from
Their burning bodies in a border war
Of gas attacks, and minefields cleared by boys.

Two and a half millennia ago
This is the seat of empire, and a king
Sits in his palace tipsy with wine and power.
He has Candaules' syndrome – that's an itch
To show his wife off to the gaping crowd
And have them lech for what they can't get near.
He summons her to put her finery on
And give the court a glimpse of what it's missing.

But Vashti is a proto-feminist:

'Tell that polygamous misogynist,'
She snaps, 'Queen Vashti is no strip-artiste
To be the last course at a drunken feast;

Inform the crapulous old fool he's kissed
His Vashti for the last time if he thinks
She'll shimmy for his cronies' leers and winks . . .'

* * *

The courtiers mitigate the message somewhat:
'Great king, thy sent-for Vashti will not come.'
'Will not come?!' The king's embarrassed, glances round,
A weak smile on his shiny lips. A knot
Of nobles in the corner starts gesticulating –
Frowns, mutterings, more gestures, nods, and then
A smarmy spokesman with a swish of robes
Steps forward: 'My lord, this is a precedent
That cannot be permitted to proceed:
If she, the consort of God's shadow, flouts
Your royal will in this outrageous way,
There's not a wife in all of Persia who'll
Continue to obey her legal lord.
My lord, impertinence like this cannot
Remain unpunished, the fabric of society . . .'

'Enough, enough, stop! I divorce the bitch.
Satisfied? Call me a scribe, my chief scribe.
You. Ready? Take this down. Have it proclaimed
Wherever in the world my word is law . . .
"The great king in his palace in Shushan,
Lord of the rising and the setting sun
(Etcetera, etcetera – fill up the scroll
According to the usual rigmarole . . .)
Hereby announces that his erstwhile wife,
The sovereign Vashti, is divorced for life,
And that on pain of death she'll not appear

Within these palace walls while he dwells here . . . "
No wait, I'll make it stronger: "That on pain
Of death she shall not show her face again
In all our realms until her dying day . . . "
There, that'll teach the cow to disobey.'

He sinks back, sips his wine and tries to push
Away the thought that of the whole vast harem
Delicious Vashti really was the nicest . . .
What had got into her? But then he smiles,
Another thought has struck him. He will start
A search, just like a fairy-tale's, to find
A perfect, pure and pulchritudinous
Replacement; an obedient replacement.
He glances up; the scribe's still there, unsure
If he should stay or go. 'Wait, take this down too:
"Wanted, a beautiful obedient spouse
To supervise the servants, run the house
And please her lord. Race immaterial,
Must be a virgin – apply to the Imperial
Director of the Harems in Shushan.
All applications treated in strict confidence –
Ambitious parents, here's that special chance." '

* * *

Within the palace lives an exile:
One whom, till now, Fortune has favoured –
A functionary who does his job
With minute care, who lives a life
Above reproach, whose hidden heart
Slogs still, three generations gone
Before his people were brought here
As slaves to glorify the grip
Of Babylon. He's Mordecai,
And has a ward, his uncle's child,
An orphan, his obsessive joy

And chief anxiety, the brave
And modest, beautiful young Esther,
Who must marry soon . . .

She hears him out, and like the good
Girl that she is agrees; who knows
What *her* heart feels apart from pleasure
That she can please her fussy cousin?

And he's still fussing: 'Not a word though, listen dear,
Of who we are – not that there's anything to fear –
But as you know we're foreigners . . . not everyone's
Our closest friend – I hope I've made my meaning clear?'

How should we picture her?
Lost in the Louvre
Hangs Chassériau's appalling painting –
A sip of soft pornography
To titillate the palate of
The century of Emma Bovary –
Kitsch waves her *poshlost* wand
And Esther is a blue-eyed blonde,
White, nude, and putting up her hair
As if she thought she might soon dare
To try out for a chorus line
Of naked nymphets in a rude revue
(Exactly what Queen Vashti would not do)
– *The Pimp and I*, or *My Fair Concubine*.

A gaudy bauble for the king, a one-night stand?
Or someone Toussaint l'Ouverture would understand?
An ardent Jeanne d'Arc racial heroine,
Mantegna's noble antique Amazon,
Young, strong and argumentative – a force
That thrusts aside her cousin's cautious course
And puts her ardent life at risk to save
An ethnos threatened by extinction . . .

For us as she
Goes forward to the weird selection process
She's not much more than this – a woman who
Is doing what her guardian has advised.
(Who could imagine that he might pick *her*?)

* * *

But that is what he does.

What glimpse pulls back his wandering glance?
A sexy something in her stance?
Her difference? Or her diffidence?

Whatever it might be she's gone,
Proclaimed the perfect paragon,
Whisked from the sight of everyone.

* * *

Not quite. Each day her cousin Mordecai
Walks by the palace wall in hopes he'll hear
'How Esther did, what should become of her' –
The moment cuts through all the story's grandeur
(Its kings and harems and mad panoply)
As simply as a hurt child's sudden cry.

* * *

A second lucky break comes next. Not all
The courtly functionaries who wait on call
Are wholly loyal to the royal throne –
Some always feel they have good cause to moan.

And Mordecai, who's silent and discreet,
Waits in a gateway, unseen from the street;
He overhears two courtiers passing by

Plotting just how and where the king must die.

Soon Esther knows – immediately she's said it
She sees the king gives Mordecai the credit.

* * *

But enter now the specious malcontent –
We've seen him dribbling his foul effluent
In every country worthy of the name;
His tactics stay insidious and the same,

Keen to persuade his restive government
Strangers are certainly the instrument
Of forces sent to rot our national fibre
(This *canard* works from Kansas to the Khyber),

They're agents up to something violent –
Subversive, anti-us, malevolent,
Corrosive of our honour and our morals,
Weakening our will with their divisive quarrels,

Un-Persian, un-American, un-Greek . . .
Appeals to join our patriotic clique
And rid the land of towel-heads, spics or queers
Have never yet descended on deaf ears.

One such is Haman, who intones his fears,
His patriotic, loyal and moral fears,
Into his monarch's wine-befuddled ears.

* * *

'My lord I'd like to bring to your attention
A subject that it's difficult to mention
Taking all views into consideration
The foreign and domestic situation

Your empire's safety, honour and stability
Your humble servant's minimal ability . . .'

'Haman, what have you got to say?'

'It's well known that a man can't serve two masters
And several national scandalous disasters
Have come about because of ethnic latitude –
They could have been avoided with an attitude
That's shall we say more . . .'

'Haman, what have you got to say?'

'The Jews my lord.'

'The Jews? What of them? Who are they?'

'Your subjects, some of them, but there's the problem as it were my lord, they're here but also there, untrustworthy, one doesn't quite know where . . .'

'My subjects then? See that you leave my subjects be.'

'But that's just it my lord – your interests and the interests of the empire ever foremost in my mind – one doesn't know where their allegiances reside, they have their own laws and don't follow ours, besides they're very secretive and where they live you know, well I don't credit foolish rumours but some people say, reliable informants normally, that children disappear, absurd of course but there one is, it doesn't do to have a separate self-controlling group within your realm my lord, some might say it's a threat, a challenge, an encroachment on your power, absurd of course as if there could be such a thing, but there one is and most of all they're not like us, no not at all, I mean it's obvious, they've different laws and secret customs, God knows what they're up to in those meeting places . . .'

'My subjects then?'

'In name, in name alone my lord but who knows who they're ready to rise up for in reality, and they are rich my lord with money that is yours by right and would be yours if they were driven out or otherwise eliminated, but the nub my lord is they're an alien race and not at all like us, despising us in fact, and ethnic differences are ethnic differences there's no denying that, a threat to unity, subversion of the single state which centres on your majesty, a dark stain to be cleansed . . .'

'A threat? How so?'

'An unknown quantity my lord, too rich, too powerful, and uncontrollable while they're alive, they should be cleansed if we're to keep our former greatness, cleansed . . .'

'Cleansed?'

'Killed.'

'Kill them. Decide the date. See not one's left alive.'

* * *

The scene is set
As if it were
An endless loop
Of silent film
That flickers on
Grainy grotesque
Through centuries

The silence is unbroken by their screams
The hooves and tanks allow no amnesty

The child is marched out with his hands held high
The pile of bodies topples to the pit

* * *

An order goes out from the palace:
The land is to be scoured
The Jews are now non-people
Their property impounded.
Haman's the happiest of men.

And Mordecai, the careful
Husbander of chances, sees
In one fell whirlwind all
His plans and calculations
Disperse like storm-blown sand.

* * *

Now ritual is left him and he mourns –
In public, cries his loud and bitter cry,
Wailing not as a harbinger who warns
But as an emblem that his people die.

Loudly he mourns before the palace gate,
A figure clothed in sackcloth, smeared with ash –
One who was fortunate and almost great
Now grovels on the ground beneath Fate's lash.

Her maids tell Esther of her cousin's cries
And she in consternation sends to know
What's brought him there in this unnatural guise,
The cause of his apocalyptic woe.

He hands her messenger the royal page
That spells their death, then clutches at a straw:

Esther can mitigate their sovereign's rage,
She will, if anyone, rewrite his law.

Esther pleads protocol – she cannot break
The court's rule that no man unsummoned may
Approach the royal throne; her life's at stake
Since it is certain death to disobey.

'And it is certain death to hesitate,'
He answers her – 'Esther cannot avoid
The king's decree that in the Persian state
Every last living Jew shall be destroyed.'

'We'll fast three days,' she says, 'then I will try
To move the heart of him who said he'd cherish
My life above his own – unbidden I
Will go, and if I perish, then I perish.'

* * *

The three days pass, and Esther waits
Within the king's gaze, if his glance . . .

She sees he sees her and her heart
Stands still a moment till he smiles
And stretches out his sceptre as
The sign she may approach: 'My Queen,
My consort and my life, what is it?
I see a question in your eyes –
Say what you long for and it's yours
To half the kingdom.'
'Lord, I desire
That you and Haman grace my palace
With your presence, and eat the banquet
I and my maids have set for you.'

They banqueted as she had asked,
But when the king, who saw that something
Still troubled her, repeated his
Request, she too repeated hers,
That he and Haman once more come
The next day to her rooms to feast.

Now Haman bustles home (and almost stumbles
Over the silent Mordecai who sits
Unmoving by the palace gate as if
He did not see the outer world
And only lived within his mind).

The fat fool enters with a clap of hands
And shouts out to his flustered wife:
'My dear, you'll never guess who dined
Alone with Esther and the king today – I did!
Darling, you'll never guess who'll dine
Alone with them tomorrow too – I will!
Honey, you'll never guess who's now
The favourite courtier of our lovely queen – I am!'

'What did you do to that poor lonely Esther?
You flattered her? You kissed her? You caressed her?
When Haman smiles what woman can resist?
Now come here naughty Haman and be kissed.'

* * *

That night the king is worried and can't sleep.
He sends off to the archives where they keep
Records of all the sovereign's said and done;
A scribe reads dull events through one by one
Until among the bland minutiae
He reaches treachery and Mordecai.
'Stop there,' the king says, and sits up in bed.
'Now if it weren't for him I would be dead.

What did we do for him? Is it recorded
Exactly how his loyalty was rewarded?'
The scribe reads silently, then, 'No my lord,
There's nothing noted down here, not a word.'
'Call Haman to me' – and when Haman's there,
'Suggest a present that I might prepare
For someone's who's especially dear to me.'
And Haman, who thinks, 'It can only be
Myself he means', simpers and says, 'My lord,
Your clothes, your horse, would be a fit reward –
Then let the lucky man ride through the town
Where all can see his glory and bow down.'
'I like it,' says the king, 'Deliver my
Best horse and royal robes to Mordecai.'

* * *

A setback for him, so he thinks, but still
He has his sovereign's and his queen's goodwill
And surely at her second banquet he
Will be rewarded too, appropriately.

The feast begins, and goes on for two days –
Wine makes the world an undeciphered haze;
Again the king asks Esther what request
Presses against her heart still unexpressed.

Now is the moment and she hears her voice
Say, 'Since you ask me and I have no choice,
I beg you as your queen and as your wife
To give me what I gave to you, my life;

And more, to give my people's lives to them;
Revoke, my lord, the orders that condemn
My kinsfolk to destruction and despair.'
The king starts up in fury: 'Who would dare,'

He bawls, 'to lift a hand against my queen?'
'Your trusted intimate, who stood between
The world and you – it's Haman I accuse
Of plotting the destruction of the Jews

Of whom I, Esther, your loved queen, am one.'
Tableau! The king turns on his heel, he's gone
To pace his garden, he needs air and space;
Now Haman throws himself upon his face

At Esther's feet, half rises, tries to seize
Her hand, her hem, grabs wildly for her knees . . .
And in the midst of this ungainly sprawling
The king returns to see his servant mauling

– It seems – his queen. 'Get this man out of here,'
He screams, 'The idiot's not content to smear
My subjects with his slanderous filth and lies,
He tries to rape my queen before my eyes!'

And Haman's hanged upon the gallows he'd
Had built for Mordecai; all he's decreed
Is quashed. On whom now will the king rely
In Haman's place? Why, who but Mordecai . . .

The good win out at last, the evil fail;
I said this story was a fairy-tale.

* * *

A fairy-tale that has a coda though
As painful as a scorpion's, since its sting's
More harsh than anything that hides within
Even the grimmest bits of Grimm.

Revenge becomes the order of the day.
First Haman's relatives are swept away –

His silly wife, who's no great loss, it's true,
But then his children are all murdered too,
And not content with that the word goes out
That every adult, every child, throughout
The kingdom who's declared their enemy
The Jews may slaughter . . . and they do.
A story
Which was comic, comforting, in that we knew
The end was to be happy, is again
A tale of death, revenge delighted in,
Pillage and murder now made licit since
When our side does it, it's another matter
And doesn't count, I mean they asked for it,
Especially the children.

* * *

Too atavistic, tribal, now the tale
Twists from our hands as if it were a live thing
Unwilling to be tamed at our discretion.

* * *

The long chain reaches back – here's Ezra's voice,
And Nehemiah's, ensuring that the stock
Stays pure, and not above a little local
Judiciously applied persuasion either,
Strangers denounced and beaten, driven out,
The precious tribal purity preserved . . .

The long chain reaches forward, snakes its way
Through centuries of loathing down to us,
And of the million sites I name but one:

Medieval York, the town I loved in childhood,
Where I began this tale and where within
My lifetime Jews would leave the train one stop

Before and so not pass through somewhere made
Anathema forever by what happened
Eight hundred years ago, still resonant,
Still real, recorded soberly in Hebrew
Stark at the foot of Clifford's Tower, which looks
To be a fantasy of merry England,
A gothic folly on a grassy knoll,
That once became another Golgotha –
The site of England's last, most ruthless pogrom.

Not only where I write but when: once more
The tribes are arming in their separate ghettoes,
Eager for Armageddon, ethnic cleansing,
Final solutions to the endless list
Of ineradicable hatreds we
Inherit, cherish, thrive on: solutions to
The one recurring problem of our race,
That we are all too inescapably,
Too evilly, the same.

* * *

Envoi

This story's old and always new,
A burden that won't go away,
These things can't happen but they do.

The raped are women whom we knew
The orphans kids we helped to play;
This story's old and always new.

The tortured are our neighbours who
We didn't really want to stay;
These things can't happen but they do.

And ethnic cleansing could mean you
(Skins, Nazis or the KKK),
This story's old and always new.

Survivors of each racial coup
Vow to remember and repay,
These things can't happen but they do.

The dispossessed know this is true;
Hatred, not love, will find a way –
This story's old and always new;
These things can't happen but they do.

They do.

York, England, May 1993–Columbus, Ohio, August 1993

NOTE

The epigraph is from a letter by Freya Stark, dated 30 April 1930, and is included in volume II of her autobiography, *Beyond Euphrates*. The paintings referred to are by Chassériau (1819–1856), *La Toilette d'Esther*, now in the Louvre; and by Mantegna (1431–1506), *Esther and Mordecai*, now in the Cincinnati Art Museum. The poem incorporates one line of Emblem VI, Book IV, of the *Emblems* of Francis Quarles (1592–1644), and a few phrases from the King James translation of the Bible. The York pogrom occurred in April 1190. Those who escaped the first fury of the mob barricaded themselves in a fortified keep called Clifford's Tower; this was eventually stormed and the surviving Jewish population of the city was slaughtered.